Cuban Economic Misery: Debunking the US Blockade Myth

Copyright Page

TITLE: Cuban Economic Misery: Deb unking the US Blockade Myth

1ST Edition

Copyright @ 2023

ISBN: 9798223720683

Table of Contents

Cuban Economic Misery: Debunking the Blockade Myth

By Roberto Miguel Rodriguez

Chapter 1: Introduction

Background and significance of the topic

Cuba, a country known for its socialist regime and strained relationship with the United States, has long been plagued by economic struggles and hardships. The subchapter "Background and significance of the topic" aims to provide scholars and economists with a comprehensive understanding of the factors contributing to Cuban economic misery, debunking the commonly held belief that it is solely due to the US blockage. By exploring various aspects such as mismanagement, corruption, brain drain, centralized planning, agriculture, economic disparity, limited foreign investment, the black market, and limited access to technology, this subchapter sheds light on the true causes of Cuba's economic troubles.

One of the main factors contributing to Cuba's economic misery is the mismanagement and incapacity of its leaders. Despite the country's rich resources and potential, ineffective policies, poor decision-making, and corruption have hindered economic growth and development. Scholars and economists need to understand this crucial aspect to accurately analyze and propose solutions to alleviate Cuba's economic woes.

Corruption has also had a significant impact on the Cuban economy. Rampant corruption within the government and state-owned enterprises has siphoned off funds meant for public welfare, infrastructure development, and economic growth. This subchapter examines how corruption has hindered investment, discouraged foreign businesses, and perpetuated economic inequality.

Inflation and hyperinflation are pressing issues in Cuba. The subchapter delves into the causes and consequences of these economic phenomena, exploring their impact on the everyday lives of Cuban citizens and businesses. It also highlights the role of centralized planning, which has stifled innovation, efficiency, and productivity, further exacerbating inflationary pressures.

Brain drain, the mass emigration of highly skilled individuals, has had a detrimental effect on Cuba's economy. The subchapter analyzes how the loss of talented professionals in various fields, such as medicine and technology, has created significant human capital deficiencies and hindered economic growth.

The limited access to foreign investment has also been a significant obstacle for Cuba's economic development. It investigates the consequences of stringent regulations and policies that have deterred foreign businesses from investing in Cuba, hindering job creation, technological advancements, and economic diversification.

Furthermore, the subchapter explores the role of the black market and informal economy in Cuba. It examines how these underground economic activities have thrived due to limited opportunities in the formal sector, contributing to the overall economic disparity and inequality within the country.

Lastly, this subchapter addresses the economic consequences of limited access to technology and the internet in Cuba. It evaluates how restricted access to modern technology and the internet has hindered innovation, productivity, and global competitiveness.

By thoroughly examining these topics, scholars and economists can gain a nuanced understanding of the root causes of Cuban economic misery, moving beyond the simplistic notion of solely blaming the US blockage. This subchapter aims to contribute to a more informed and comprehensive discussion on the challenges faced by Cuba and potential solutions to improve its economic trajectory.

Research objectives

The subchapter "Research Objectives" aims to provide an in-depth analysis of the key research areas that will be explored in the book "Cuban Economic Misery: Debunking the US Blockage Myth." This section will outline the specific objectives and questions that will guide the research, addressing the concerns of scholars and economists interested in understanding the root causes of Cuba's economic difficulties.

1. Cuban Economic Misery: Not Because of US Blockage but Because of Leaders' Mismanagement and Incapacity:

This objective aims to examine the role of mismanagement and incapacity of Cuban leaders in the economic hardships faced by the country. The research will analyze various economic policies implemented by the Cuban government and their impact on economic development.

2. Impact of Corruption on the Cuban Economy:

This objective aims to investigate the extent and consequences of corruption within the Cuban economy. The research will explore the ways in which corruption hampers economic growth, stifles foreign investment, and exacerbates economic inequality.

3. Inflation and Hyperinflation in Cuba:

This objective aims to analyze the factors contributing to inflation and hyperinflation in Cuba. The research will examine the impact of government policies, currency devaluation, and price controls on the purchasing power of the Cuban population.

4. Economic Impact of Brain Drain in Cuba:

This objective aims to assess the economic consequences of brain drain on Cuba's development. The research will investigate the factors that drive skilled professionals to leave the country and the subsequent impact on sectors such as healthcare, education, and innovation.

5. Effects of Centralized Planning on the Cuban Economy:

This objective aims to evaluate the economic consequences of Cuba's centralized planning system. The research will examine the efficiency of resource allocation, the stifling effect on entrepreneurship, and the impact on productivity and economic growth.

6. Cuban Agriculture and Food Scarcity:

This objective aims to explore the challenges faced by Cuba's agricultural sector and its impact on food scarcity. The research will investigate the reasons behind the country's dependence on food imports, the inefficiencies in agricultural production, and the potential for sustainable solutions.

7. Economic Disparity and Inequality in Cuba:

This objective aims to analyze the extent and causes of economic disparity and inequality within Cuban society. The research will investigate the impact of government policies, limited access to economic opportunities, and the concentration of wealth in certain sectors.

8. Economic Impact of Limited Foreign Investment in Cuba:

This objective aims to examine the consequences of limited foreign investment in Cuba. The research will explore the barriers that prevent foreign businesses from entering the Cuban market, the impact on job creation and economic growth, and the potential benefits of increased foreign investment.

9. Role of Black Market and Informal Economy in Cuba:

This objective aims to understand the role of the black market and informal economy in Cuba's economic landscape. The research will analyze the motivations behind informal economic activities, the impact on government revenue, and the potential for formalization and regulation.

10. Economic Consequences of Limited Access to Technology and Internet in Cuba:

This objective aims to assess the economic implications of limited access to technology and the internet in Cuba. The research will explore the impact on innovation, entrepreneurship, education, and productivity, as well as the potential benefits of increased technological connectivity.

By addressing these research objectives, the book seeks to provide a comprehensive analysis of the factors contributing to Cuba's economic misery, debunking the myth that the US blockade is solely responsible. Scholars and economists will find this subchapter particularly valuable as it lays the foundation for a rigorous examination of the Cuban economy and its underlying challenges.

Methodology

In this subchapter, we will outline the methodology used in the research and analysis conducted for the book "Cuban Economic Misery: Debunking the US Blockage Myth." The objective of this book is to provide scholars and economists with a comprehensive understanding of the factors contributing to the economic hardships faced by Cuba, which are often erroneously attributed to the US blockade. By debunking this myth, we aim to shed light on the real causes of Cuban economic misery.

To achieve this goal, a multidisciplinary approach was adopted, combining qualitative and quantitative research methods. Extensive literature reviews were conducted to gather information on the various aspects of the Cuban economy, including its history, policies, and current state. This allowed us to establish a solid foundation for our analysis.

Primary research was also conducted to supplement the existing literature. Interviews were conducted with experts in the field, including scholars, economists, and individuals with first-hand experience of the Cuban economy. These interviews provided valuable insights and perspectives, helping us to develop a comprehensive understanding of the issues at hand.

Data analysis played a crucial role in our research. Statistical data on key economic indicators, such as GDP, inflation rates, and foreign investment, was collected and analyzed. This allowed us to identify trends and patterns, as well as to quantify the impact of certain factors on the Cuban economy.

Case studies were also utilized to provide real-life examples and illustrate the economic consequences of certain policies. These case studies included topics such as the impact of corruption on the Cuban economy, the effects of brain drain and limited foreign investment, and the role of the black market and informal economy.

Lastly, comparative analysis was conducted to provide a broader perspective on the Cuban economy. By examining the experiences of other countries facing similar challenges, we were able to draw meaningful comparisons and identify potential solutions.

It is important to note that while every effort was made to ensure the accuracy and reliability of the information presented in this book, limitations exist. The Cuban economy is a complex and dynamic system, influenced by a multitude of factors. Therefore, this book should be viewed as a comprehensive analysis rather than an exhaustive account.

Chapter 2: Understanding Cuban Economic Misery

Historical overview of Cuban economy

The history of the Cuban economy is a complex and intriguing one, marked by significant events and policies that have shaped its trajectory. Understanding this historical context is crucial to debunking the myth that the economic misery in Cuba is solely a result of the US blockade. This subchapter aims to provide scholars and economists with a comprehensive overview of the historical factors that have contributed to the current state of the Cuban economy.

One of the key factors that have hindered Cuba's economic growth is the mismanagement and incapacity of its leaders. From the early days of the Cuban Revolution, the government adopted a centralized planning model, which aimed to redistribute wealth and create a socialist society. However, this approach led to the concentration of power in the hands of a few, resulting in inefficiencies, corruption, and economic stagnation.

Corruption has also had a significant impact on the Cuban economy. Over the years, a culture of bribery and embezzlement has emerged, diverting resources away from productive sectors and undermining public trust in the government. This has further exacerbated the economic hardships faced by ordinary Cubans.

Inflation and hyperinflation have plagued the Cuban economy, leading to a decline in purchasing power and a rise in prices. The government's excessive printing of money to finance its budget deficits, coupled with the lack of productive investment, has fueled this inflationary spiral.

The brain drain phenomenon has had severe economic consequences for Cuba. The loss of skilled professionals and talented individuals to emigration has created a significant human capital deficit, hindering economic development and innovation.

Centralized planning, while intended to promote equality, has stifled incentives for entrepreneurship and private sector growth. This has led to a lack of dynamism and innovation in the Cuban economy, with state-owned enterprises dominating most sectors.

Cuban agriculture has been plagued by inefficiencies and outdated practices, leading to food scarcity and reliance on imports. The government's control over land and production decisions has limited the ability of farmers to respond to market demands and invest in modern techniques.

Economic disparity and inequality have been persistent issues in Cuba. While the government has made efforts to reduce poverty, the gap between the rich and the poor remains significant, with access to resources and opportunities heavily influenced by political connections.

Limited foreign investment has also hindered Cuba's economic growth. The US blockade, while a contributing factor, is not the sole reason for this limitation. Cuba's restrictive investment laws, lack of legal protections, and bureaucratic hurdles have discouraged foreign investors from entering the market.

The black market and informal economy have played a crucial role in sustaining the livelihoods of many Cubans. However, reliance on these sectors has hindered formal economic growth and perpetuated inequalities.

Limited access to technology and the internet has further isolated Cuba from the global economy. The lack of connectivity has hindered innovation, entrepreneurship, and access to information, impeding economic development.

In conclusion, the historical overview of the Cuban economy reveals that the economic misery experienced by the country cannot be solely attributed to the US blockade. Rather, factors such as leaders' mismanagement and incapacity, corruption, inflation, brain drain, centralized planning, agricultural challenges, economic disparity, limited foreign investment, reliance on the black market, and restricted access to technology have all played significant roles. Understanding these complexities is crucial for scholars and economists seeking to analyze and propose solutions to address Cuba's economic challenges.

Factors contributing to Cuban economic crisis

Introduction:

Cuba has experienced a prolonged economic crisis that has significantly impacted the standard of living for its citizens. Despite claims that the United States blockade is solely responsible for this crisis, a closer examination reveals that the economic troubles in Cuba stem from a combination of mismanagement and incapacity by the country's leaders. This subchapter aims to shed light on the various factors contributing to the Cuban economic crisis, providing scholars and economists with a comprehensive analysis.

1. Impact of Corruption on Cuban Economy:

Corruption has plagued the Cuban economy, diverting resources away from productive sectors and hindering economic growth. Misallocation of funds and lack of transparency have weakened the state's ability to effectively manage the economy, resulting in widespread economic decline.

2. Inflation and Hyperinflation in Cuba:

Poor economic policies, such as excessive money printing and price controls, have led to rampant inflation and, at times, hyperinflation. This has eroded the purchasing power of the Cuban peso, exacerbating the economic woes faced by the population.

3. Economic Impact of Brain Drain in Cuba:

The emigration of skilled professionals and intellectuals, known as brain drain, has had severe economic consequences for Cuba. The loss of human capital has hindered innovation and productivity, further impeding the country's economic development.

4. Effects of Centralized Planning on Cuban Economy:

Cuba's centrally planned economy has stifled entrepreneurship and hindered economic growth. The lack of market mechanisms and excessive state control have resulted in inefficiencies, low productivity, and a failure to adapt to changing global economic trends.

5. Cuban Agriculture and Food Scarcity:

Decades of mismanagement and insufficient investment in the agricultural sector have led to chronic food scarcity in Cuba. The reliance on outdated farming techniques, limited access to agricultural inputs, and inadequate infrastructure have all contributed to the country's struggle to feed its population.

6. Economic Disparity and Inequality in Cuba:

Despite claims of an egalitarian society, Cuba experiences significant economic disparity and inequality. The state's control over key sectors of the economy has allowed certain elites to accumulate wealth, while the majority of the population suffers from limited economic opportunities and access to basic necessities.

7. Economic Impact of Limited Foreign Investment in Cuba:

The restrictive policies and regulations surrounding foreign investment in Cuba have deterred much-needed capital inflows. This has stifled economic growth, hindered technological advancements, and limited access to international markets.

8. Role of Black Market and Informal Economy in Cuba:

The prevalence of a black market and informal economy in Cuba highlights the failure of the state-led economic model. The need for individuals to engage in illicit activities and informal trade is a direct result of the government's inability to provide adequate economic opportunities and meet the population's needs.

9. Economic Consequences of Limited Access to Technology and Internet in Cuba:

The limited access to technology and the internet in Cuba has hindered economic development and innovation. The lack of connectivity has deprived businesses and individuals of the tools necessary for growth, limiting their ability to participate in the global economy.

Conclusion:

The Cuban economic crisis is not solely a result of the US blockade but rather a culmination of factors such as mismanagement, corruption, brain drain, centralized planning, limited foreign investment, and technological constraints. Understanding these factors is crucial for scholars and economists seeking to accurately analyze and address the root causes of Cuba's economic struggles. By debunking the myth of the US blockade as the sole cause, it becomes apparent that Cuba's economic recovery requires comprehensive reforms and a shift away from failed economic policies.

Debunking the US blockage myth

Introduction:

The misconception that the United States' blockade is solely responsible for Cuba's economic misery has been widely perpetuated. However, a deeper analysis reveals that Cuban economic woes are primarily a result of mismanagement and incapacity on the part of its leaders. This chapter aims to address this fallacy and shed light on the true factors that have contributed to Cuba's economic struggles.

Leaders Mismanagement and Incapacity:

One of the key reasons for Cuba's economic misery lies in the mismanagement and incapacity of its leaders. The Cuban government's centralized planning approach and inefficient bureaucracy have hindered economic growth and development. Poor decision-making, lack of accountability, and rampant corruption have further exacerbated the situation, diverting resources away from productive sectors and into the hands of corrupt officials.

Impact of Corruption on Cuban Economy:

Corruption has had a devastating impact on the Cuban economy. It has hindered foreign investment, discouraged entrepreneurship, and perpetuated a culture of economic inequality. The misallocation of resources due to corruption has led to a lack of investment in vital sectors, such as healthcare and education, exacerbating the economic hardship faced by the Cuban people.

Inflation and Hyperinflation in Cuba:

Another significant factor contributing to Cuba's economic misery is rampant inflation and hyperinflation. Poor economic policies, such as excessive money printing, have eroded the value of the Cuban peso, resulting in skyrocketing prices for essential goods and services. This has severely affected the purchasing power of the Cuban population, leading to widespread poverty and economic instability.

Economic Impact of Brain Drain in Cuba:

Cuba has experienced a significant brain drain as skilled professionals seek better opportunities abroad. The loss of talented individuals in sectors such as healthcare and engineering has further crippled the country's economy. The exodus of skilled labor has left a void that the Cuban government has been unable to fill, resulting in a decline in productivity and innovation.

Effects of Centralized Planning on Cuban Economy:

The Cuban government's adherence to a centrally planned economy has stifled economic growth and development. The lack of market-driven mechanisms and excessive government control have hindered entrepreneurship and innovation. This top-down approach has failed to incentivize productivity and has contributed to the country's economic stagnation.

Conclusion:

Contrary to popular belief, the US blockade is not the sole cause of Cuba's economic misery. The mismanagement and incapacity of its leaders, rampant corruption, inflation, brain drain, limited foreign investment, centralized planning, and other factors have played a significant role in the country's economic decline. Understanding these underlying issues is crucial for scholars and economists to develop effective strategies and policies that can help alleviate Cuba's economic woes and pave the way for sustainable growth and prosperity.

Chapter 3: Cuban Economic Misery: Leadership Mismanagement and Incapacity

Role of leadership in economic decision-making

Leadership plays a crucial role in economic decision-making, shaping the trajectory of a nation's economy and determining its success or failure. In the case of Cuba, the country's economic misery is not solely a result of the US blockade, as commonly believed, but rather a consequence of leaders' mismanagement and incapacity. This subchapter will delve into the various aspects of leadership's impact on Cuba's economy, shedding light on the root causes of the nation's economic struggles.

One significant factor contributing to Cuba's economic woes is the pervasive impact of corruption. Leaders entrusted with decision-making powers often prioritize personal gain over the well-being of the country, leading to misallocation of resources and hindered economic growth. By examining the role of corruption in Cuba's economy, scholars and economists can gain a deeper understanding of the systemic challenges that impede progress.

Furthermore, inflation and hyperinflation have plagued the Cuban economy, exacerbating the hardships faced by its citizens. Leaders' mismanagement of monetary policies, excessive government spending, and lack of effective economic planning have contributed to the erosion of the Cuban currency's value. This subchapter will explore the causes and consequences of inflation and hyperinflation in Cuba, highlighting the detrimental effects on the overall economic stability.

The brain drain phenomenon, driven by leaders' mismanagement, has had a significant economic impact on Cuba. The loss of skilled professionals and intellectuals due to limited opportunities and political constraints has resulted in a dearth of talent and expertise within the country. Scholars and economists will gain insights into the consequences of brain drain on Cuba's economy, including reduced innovation, productivity, and human capital development.

Additionally, the effects of centralized planning on the Cuban economy cannot be overlooked. The leadership's control over economic decision-making processes has led to inefficiencies, lack of flexibility, and a stifling of entrepreneurial initiatives. This subchapter will analyze the consequences of centralized planning, shedding light on its detrimental effects on Cuba's economic growth and development.

Other subtopics that will be explored in this chapter include Cuban agriculture and food scarcity, economic disparity and inequality, limited foreign investment, the role of the black market and informal economy, as well as the economic consequences of limited access to technology and the internet.

By examining the role of leadership in economic decision-making, this subchapter aims to debunk the myth that Cuba's economic misery is solely due to the US blockade. Through a comprehensive analysis of the various factors at play, scholars and economists can gain a nuanced understanding of the root causes of Cuba's economic challenges and propose potential solutions to alleviate its economic hardships.

Impact of mismanagement on Cuban economy

Mismanagement and economic miseries have plagued the Cuban economy for decades. Contrary to popular belief, the economic struggles faced by the Cuban people cannot be solely attributed to the US blockade. Instead, it is the result of leaders' mismanagement and their incapacity to effectively address the challenges faced by the nation.

One of the key impacts of mismanagement on the Cuban economy is corruption. Widespread corruption has hindered economic growth and investment, as resources are siphoned off by corrupt officials instead of being used for public welfare and development. This leads to a lack of trust in the government and discourages both domestic and foreign investors from engaging in the Cuban economy.

Inflation and hyperinflation have also plagued the Cuban economy due to mismanagement. Poor economic policies and misallocation of resources have led to rampant inflation, making it difficult for the average Cuban to afford basic necessities. The government's inability to control inflation further exacerbates the economic hardships faced by the population.

The brain drain phenomenon has had a significant economic impact on Cuba. The country has witnessed a mass exodus of highly skilled professionals seeking better opportunities abroad due to the lack of economic prospects at home. This brain drain further hampers economic growth and development, as the loss of skilled labor stifles innovation and productivity within the country.

Centralized planning has also had detrimental effects on the Cuban economy. The top-down approach to economic decision-making has stifled entrepreneurship and inhibited market dynamics, leading to inefficiencies and a lack of economic diversification. The overreliance on central planning has hindered the ability of the Cuban economy to adapt to changing global trends and has resulted in a stagnant and uncompetitive economic environment.

Furthermore, the mismanagement of the Cuban agriculture sector has contributed to food scarcity and insecurity. Inefficient agricultural practices, lack of investment, and insufficient access to modern technologies have resulted in low agricultural productivity and an inability to meet the food demands of the population. This has led to increased dependence on food imports, further straining the already struggling economy.

Economic disparity and inequality have also been exacerbated by mismanagement. The Cuban government's limited focus on income distribution and social welfare programs has resulted in a widening wealth gap, with a small elite benefiting disproportionately from the country's resources. This economic inequality further exacerbates social tensions and hampers overall economic progress.

Limited foreign investment, due to mismanagement and an unfavorable business environment, has hindered economic growth in Cuba. The government's restrictive policies and lack of transparency have deterred foreign investors, leading to a scarcity of capital and technology needed for economic development.

The role of the black market and informal economy cannot be ignored when discussing the impact of mismanagement on the Cuban economy. The lack of economic opportunities and restrictive policies have forced many Cubans to engage in informal economic activities to make ends meet. However, this unregulated sector further contributes to economic instability and hinders formal economic growth.

Lastly, limited access to technology and the internet has had severe economic consequences for Cuba. The government's tight control over information technology and limited infrastructure development have hindered the country's ability to fully participate in the digital economy. This has resulted in missed opportunities for innovation, productivity gains, and integration into global markets.

In conclusion, the impact of mismanagement on the Cuban economy is undeniable. The misallocation of resources, corruption, inflation, brain drain, centralized planning, agricultural mismanagement, economic disparity, limited foreign investment, the role of the black market, and limited access to technology have all contributed to the economic misery faced by the Cuban people. It is imperative for scholars and economists to acknowledge these factors and seek alternative strategies to address the economic challenges faced by Cuba.

Ineffectiveness of economic policies

Introduction:

The subchapter titled "Ineffectiveness of economic policies" delves into the various factors contributing to the economic misery in Cuba, debunking the myth that the US blockade is solely responsible. This chapter aims to provide scholars and economists with an in-depth analysis of the Cuban economic landscape, highlighting the mismanagement and capacity issues of the Cuban leadership that have led to the current state of affairs.

The Impact of Corruption on the Cuban Economy:

Corruption has plagued the Cuban economy, hindering its growth and impeding the effectiveness of economic policies. Scholars and economists have long argued that corrupt practices, such as embezzlement, bribery, and nepotism, have eroded public trust, discouraged foreign investment, and distorted market competition. This chapter explores the detrimental effects of corruption on the Cuban economy and calls for stricter measures to combat this pervasive issue.

Inflation and Hyperinflation in Cuba:

The persistent inflation and sporadic episodes of hyperinflation in Cuba have significantly undermined the effectiveness of economic policies. Scholars and economists have attributed these inflationary pressures to excessive government spending, inadequate monetary policies, and a lack of market-oriented reforms. This subchapter examines the root causes of inflation in Cuba and its devastating consequences on the standard of living for the Cuban people.

Economic Impact of Brain Drain in Cuba:

The exodus of skilled professionals and intellectuals from Cuba has had a profound economic impact on the country. The brain drain phenomenon, driven by limited opportunities, low wages, and political restrictions, has resulted in a significant loss of human capital. This chapter analyzes the consequences of brain drain on the Cuban economy, from a shortage of skilled labor to diminished innovation and productivity.

Effects of Centralized Planning on the Cuban Economy:

Centralized planning, a hallmark of the Cuban economic system, has stifled economic growth and impeded the effectiveness of policies. This subchapter explores the shortcomings of centralized planning, such as inefficiency, lack of responsiveness to market signals, and the failure to allocate resources effectively. Scholars and economists provide insights into the necessity of decentralization and market-oriented reforms to revitalize the Cuban economy.

Cuban Agriculture and Food Scarcity:

The Cuban agricultural sector has long struggled with inefficiencies and low productivity, leading to food scarcity and dependency on imports. Scholars and economists examine the reasons behind these challenges, including outdated farming practices, limited access to modern technology, and government regulations. This subchapter highlights the need for agrarian reforms and investments in the agricultural sector to address food scarcity in Cuba.

Conclusion:

The subchapter "Ineffectiveness of economic policies" sheds light on the multifaceted reasons behind the economic misery in Cuba. By exploring issues such as corruption, inflation, brain drain, centralized planning, agriculture, and inequality, scholars and economists gain a comprehensive understanding of the mismanagement and capacity limitations of the Cuban leadership. This chapter debunks the myth that the US blockade is solely responsible for Cuba's economic woes and emphasizes the urgent need for structural reforms to alleviate the suffering of the Cuban people and pave the way for sustainable economic growth.

Chapter 4: Impact of Corruption on Cuban Economy

Definition and types of corruption

Corruption, a pervasive issue in many societies, has had a significant impact on the Cuban economy. In this subchapter, we will explore the definition and various types of corruption that have plagued the country. Scholars and economists interested in understanding the root causes of Cuban economic misery, as well as the impact of corruption on the nation's economy, will find this section particularly informative.

Corruption can be defined as the abuse of entrusted power for personal gain or the misuse of public resources for private benefit. In Cuba, corruption manifests itself in various forms, including bribery, embezzlement, nepotism, and patronage. These corrupt practices have infiltrated various sectors, from the government to the private sector, exacerbating the economic challenges faced by the Cuban people.

Bribery, one of the most common forms of corruption, involves the provision or acceptance of money or gifts in exchange for favorable treatment or the circumvention of rules and regulations. Embezzlement, on the other hand, refers to the misappropriation of funds or assets entrusted to an individual for personal gain. These corrupt practices not only drain public resources but also undermine the trust and confidence of the Cuban people in their institutions.

Nepotism and patronage are also prevalent in Cuba, perpetuating a culture of favoritism and cronyism. Nepotism involves the appointment or advancement of family members or close associates to positions of power, often disregarding merit and qualifications. Patronage, on the other hand, refers to the exchange of political support or loyalty for rewards or favors.

The impact of corruption on the Cuban economy has been devastating. It has hindered economic growth, distorted resource allocation, and eroded public trust in institutions. Corruption has led to the mismanagement and inefficiency of state-owned enterprises, stifling innovation and productivity. Moreover, it has deterred foreign investment and hindered economic development.

In addition to corruption, other factors contribute to the economic misery in Cuba. The mismanagement and incapacity of leaders, rather than the US blockage, have played a significant role in the country's economic downfall. The impact of brain drain, inflation, hyperinflation, economic disparity, inequality, limited foreign investment, centralized planning, limited access to technology and the internet, Cuban agriculture, food scarcity, and the role of the black market and informal economy are also crucial aspects that need to be analyzed to gain a comprehensive understanding of Cuba's economic challenges.

By examining the definition and various types of corruption, scholars and economists can better comprehend the economic consequences and interplay of corruption with the other factors contributing to Cuban economic misery. Only by addressing corruption and implementing effective anti-corruption measures can Cuba hope to rebuild its economy and improve the lives of its citizens.

Corruption in Cuban government and institutions

Chapter Overview: Corruption in Cuban government and institutions is a crucial factor contributing to the economic misery experienced by the Cuban people. This subchapter aims to shed light on the impact of corruption on the Cuban economy, the effects of centralized planning, brain drain, limited foreign investment, and other related issues.

Introduction:

Corruption has long plagued the Cuban government and institutions, hindering economic growth and exacerbating the country's economic misery. Despite the prevalent narrative of blaming the US blockade for Cuba's economic struggles, it is essential to recognize the role played by leaders' mismanagement and incapacity in perpetuating this crisis.

Impact of Corruption on Cuban Economy:

Corruption permeates various aspects of the Cuban economy, leading to a lack of transparency, misallocation of resources, and inefficiencies. Bribery and embezzlement divert funds away from essential public services, hindering the provision of healthcare, education, and infrastructure development. Scholars and economists need to examine the systemic corruption within Cuban institutions and its direct impact on the economic well-being of the Cuban people.

Inflation and Hyperinflation in Cuba:

Corruption within the Cuban government and institutions has contributed to skyrocketing inflation rates and even instances of hyperinflation. The mismanagement of the economy, coupled with illicit practices and the printing of excessive amounts of money, has eroded the value of the Cuban peso, further exacerbating economic misery for the Cuban population.

Economic Impact of Brain Drain in Cuba:

The brain drain phenomenon, driven by limited opportunities, low wages, and political oppression, has a significant economic impact on Cuba. The loss of skilled professionals in sectors like medicine, engineering, and technology hampers innovation, productivity, and economic growth. Scholars and economists must explore the consequences of this brain drain on the Cuban economy and identify potential solutions.

Effects of Centralized Planning on Cuban Economy:

Cuba's centralized planning system, controlled by the government, has stifled economic growth and led to inefficiencies. The lack of market mechanisms and competition hinders productivity and innovation, perpetuating economic misery. Scholars and economists should analyze the adverse effects of this centralized planning model and propose alternative approaches that promote economic prosperity.

Conclusion:

Corruption within the Cuban government and institutions plays a pivotal role in exacerbating the economic misery faced by the Cuban people. This subchapter has highlighted the impact of corruption on the Cuban economy, as well as the consequences of centralized planning, brain drain, limited foreign investment, and other related issues. Scholars and economists must delve further into these topics to gain a comprehensive understanding of the root causes of Cuba's economic woes and contribute to finding viable solutions for a brighter future.

Economic consequences of corruption

Corruption, the abuse of power for personal gain, has had a devastating impact on the Cuban economy. Despite claims that the US blockade is the primary cause of economic misery in Cuba, it is the mismanagement and incapacity of the country's leaders that have contributed significantly to the economic decline. This subchapter explores the various ways in which corruption has hindered Cuba's economic growth, further debunking the myth of the US blockade as the sole cause of the nation's economic woes.

One of the most apparent economic consequences of corruption in Cuba is the impact on the country's public finances. Rampant corruption within governmental institutions has resulted in the misappropriation of funds, leading to a significant loss of revenue. This loss has hampered the government's ability to invest in essential infrastructure, education, healthcare, and other crucial sectors. As a result, the quality of public services has deteriorated, exacerbating the economic misery experienced by the Cuban population.

Corruption has also contributed to inflation and even hyperinflation in Cuba. When public funds are siphoned off through corrupt practices, it creates an imbalance in the economy, leading to an increase in prices. The scarcity of goods due to corruption further exacerbates inflationary pressures. As a result, the cost of living has skyrocketed, making it increasingly difficult for the average Cuban citizen to afford basic necessities.

The economic impact of brain drain in Cuba cannot be ignored. Corruption has led to a lack of opportunities and a stifling business environment, prompting many skilled professionals to seek employment abroad. This brain drain has resulted in a loss of human capital, which is essential for economic growth and innovation. The absence of skilled workers has hindered the development of industries and further perpetuated the economic misery experienced by the Cuban people.

Centralized planning has also had detrimental effects on the Cuban economy. The government's control over the means of production and resource allocation has stifled entrepreneurship and innovation. The lack of competition and incentives for productivity has resulted in inefficiencies and a decline in economic output. This centralized planning has perpetuated economic stagnation and hindered the country's ability to attract foreign investment.

Moreover, corruption has severely impacted Cuban agriculture, leading to food scarcity. Mismanagement and corruption within the agricultural sector have resulted in a decline in productivity and a reliance on expensive food imports. The lack of investment and incentives for farmers has further exacerbated the food crisis, leaving many Cubans struggling to access sufficient and affordable food.

The economic disparity and inequality within Cuba have also been exacerbated by corruption. The elite and well-connected individuals in the country have been able to exploit their positions for personal gain, while the majority of the population continues to suffer from economic misery. This inequality has widened the gap between the rich and poor, further dividing society and hindering economic progress.

Limited foreign investment in Cuba has also had significant economic consequences. Corruption and the lack of transparency within the Cuban business environment have deterred foreign investors from entering the market. The absence of foreign investment has stifled economic growth and innovation, limiting job opportunities and perpetuating the economic misery experienced by the Cuban population.

The role of the black market and informal economy cannot be overlooked in understanding the economic consequences of corruption in Cuba. The lack of legitimate employment opportunities and a stifling business environment have forced many Cubans to resort to informal and illegal activities to make ends meet. This underground economy further perpetuates corruption and undermines the formal economy, hindering economic growth and development.

Lastly, limited access to technology and the internet has had adverse economic consequences in Cuba. The lack of technological advancements and the inability to access global markets and information has hampered innovation and economic progress. This limited access to technology has further isolated Cuba from the global economy, hindering its ability to compete on an international scale.

In conclusion, corruption in Cuba has had severe economic consequences. The mismanagement and incapacity of the country's leaders, rather than the US blockade, have contributed significantly to the economic misery experienced by the Cuban population. The impact of corruption on public finances, inflation, brain drain, centralized planning, agriculture, economic disparity, limited foreign investment, the black market, limited access to technology, and the internet have hindered economic growth and perpetuated the economic decline in Cuba. It is imperative to address corruption within the country to pave the way for economic recovery and prosperity.

Chapter 5: Inflation and Hyperinflation in Cuba

Causes and effects of inflation

Inflation has been a persistent problem in the Cuban economy, with far-reaching consequences that have impacted various sectors and the lives of its citizens. This subchapter aims to shed light on the causes and effects of inflation in Cuba, illuminating the complex factors that have contributed to this economic phenomenon.

One of the primary causes of inflation in Cuba is the mismanagement and incapacity of its leaders. The Cuban government's centralized planning and interventionist policies have stifled economic growth, leading to a scarcity of goods and services. This scarcity, in turn, drives up prices as demand outstrips supply. Furthermore, the government's excessive printing of money to finance its budget deficits has fueled inflationary pressures, exacerbating the problem.

Corruption has also played a significant role in the Cuban economy, further contributing to inflation. The diversion of resources and funds intended for public investment into the pockets of corrupt officials has hindered economic development and led to a misallocation of resources. This corruption not only erodes public trust but also drives up prices as the cost of doing business increases due to bribery and kickbacks.

The brain drain, characterized by the emigration of skilled professionals, has had a detrimental impact on the Cuban economy. The loss of talented individuals, particularly in sectors such as healthcare and education, has resulted in a decline in productivity and innovation. This brain drain has limited the country's ability to generate wealth and has further exacerbated the inflationary pressures.

The effects of inflation are wide-ranging and have had a profound impact on the Cuban population. The most significant consequence is the erosion of purchasing power, as the value of money diminishes. This has led to a decline in the standard of living, with many struggling to afford basic necessities. Moreover, inflation has widened the economic disparity and inequality in Cuba, as the wealthy can better shield themselves from its effects compared to the poor and marginalized.

Inflation has also had adverse effects on key sectors such as agriculture, exacerbating food scarcity and leading to increased prices for essential food items. The limited access to technology and the internet, coupled with limited foreign investment, has further hindered economic growth and perpetuated the inflationary cycle.

In conclusion, the causes and effects of inflation in Cuba are multi-faceted, driven by a combination of mismanagement, corruption, brain drain, and limited access to technology and foreign investment. Understanding these factors is crucial for scholars and economists seeking to address the root causes of Cuban economic misery and devise sustainable solutions for its future prosperity.

Hyperinflation and its impact on the Cuban economy

Introduction:

Hyperinflation refers to a rapid and out-of-control increase in prices, leading to a loss of confidence in the currency and a sharp decline in the purchasing power of the population. This subchapter examines the phenomenon of hyperinflation and its impact on the Cuban economy. Contrary to popular belief, the root causes of hyperinflation in Cuba can be attributed to the mismanagement and incapacity of its leaders, rather than the alleged US blockage.

Hyperinflation as a Consequence of Mismanagement:

Cuba's economy has been plagued by mismanagement and inefficiency, resulting in a chronic fiscal deficit and an overreliance on printing money to finance government spending. As a result, the money supply has skyrocketed, leading to hyperinflation. The leaders' failure to implement effective economic policies, control public spending, and attract foreign investment has exacerbated the situation.

Effects of Hyperinflation:

Hyperinflation has devastating effects on the Cuban economy and its citizens. Firstly, it erodes the value of the national currency, making imports more expensive and reducing the standard of living for ordinary Cubans. Secondly, it undermines business confidence and discourages investment, hindering economic growth. The government's response to hyperinflation often includes imposing price controls and rationing, further distorting market forces and exacerbating scarcity.

The Role of Hyperinflation in Deepening Economic Misery:

Hyperinflation is a major contributor to the economic misery experienced by the Cuban population. The rising prices of essential goods and services, coupled with stagnant wages, have plunged many Cubans into poverty. The impact is particularly severe on vulnerable groups, such as the elderly and low-income families, who struggle to meet their basic needs.

Addressing Hyperinflation:

To address hyperinflation and its detrimental impact on the Cuban economy, a comprehensive set of reforms is required. These reforms should include fiscal discipline, reducing government spending, attracting foreign investment, promoting entrepreneurship, and implementing market-oriented policies. Furthermore, tackling corruption, improving governance, and enhancing transparency are crucial to restoring confidence in the economy and revitalizing economic growth.

Conclusion:

Hyperinflation in Cuba is a consequence of mismanagement and an unsustainable economic model, rather than the alleged US blockage. Its impact on the Cuban economy has been devastating, exacerbating economic misery and widening inequality. To overcome this challenge, bold reforms are necessary to restore fiscal stability, attract foreign investment, and create sustainable growth. By debunking the myth of the US blockage and addressing the root causes of economic mismanagement, Cuba can pave the way for a more prosperous future for its citizens.

Government measures to control inflation

Inflation has long been a significant challenge for the Cuban economy, impacting the lives of its citizens and hindering economic growth. In response, the government has implemented various measures to control inflation and stabilize prices. This subchapter explores the government's efforts to combat inflation and their effectiveness in addressing this economic issue.

One of the primary measures taken by the Cuban government to control inflation is the implementation of monetary policies. The government has employed strict control over the money supply, including limiting the printing of new currency and regulating interest rates. By managing the money supply, the government aims to prevent excessive inflationary pressures and maintain price stability.

Another key government measure is the control of prices for essential goods and services. The government sets price ceilings and monitors market prices to prevent excessive price increases. This is particularly crucial for basic necessities such as food, healthcare, and utilities, as rising prices in these sectors can have a severe impact on the population.

Additionally, the government has implemented wage controls to manage inflation. By controlling wage increases, the government aims to prevent a wage-price spiral, where higher wages lead to increased production costs and, subsequently, higher prices. This measure is designed to maintain price stability and prevent inflationary pressures from escalating.

Furthermore, the government has focused on improving productivity and efficiency in key sectors of the economy. By investing in infrastructure, technology, and human capital, the government aims to enhance production capabilities and reduce production costs. This, in turn, can help control inflation by ensuring a stable supply of goods and services at reasonable prices.

However, while these measures are undoubtedly important, it is crucial to acknowledge that the root causes of inflation in Cuba extend beyond government actions. Factors such as corruption, brain drain, economic disparity, limited foreign investment, and technological limitations all contribute to the inflationary pressures faced by the Cuban economy.

In conclusion, the Cuban government has implemented various measures to control inflation and stabilize prices. These include monetary policies, price controls, wage controls, and efforts to improve productivity. While these measures are necessary, it is vital to address the underlying causes of inflation to achieve long-lasting stability and economic growth. By tackling corruption, promoting equality, attracting foreign investment, and embracing technological advancements, the Cuban government can effectively combat inflation and create a more prosperous future for its citizens.

Chapter 6: Economic Impact of Brain Drain in Cuba

Brain drain and its implications for the economy

Subchapter: Brain Drain and its Implications for the Economy

Brain drain refers to the emigration of highly skilled or educated individuals from a country, often to seek better opportunities elsewhere. In the case of Cuba, brain drain has had significant implications for the country's economy. This subchapter aims to explore the impact of brain drain on Cuba's economic development and shed light on the underlying causes.

Cuba has long been known for its highly educated population, with a strong emphasis on free education and healthcare. However, due to economic hardships and limited opportunities, many skilled professionals and intellectuals have chosen to leave the country in search of better prospects abroad. This brain drain has resulted in a loss of human capital, expertise, and innovation, which has severely hampered Cuba's economic growth.

The implications of brain drain on the Cuban economy are far-reaching. Firstly, it creates a shortage of skilled professionals in key sectors such as healthcare, engineering, and technology. This scarcity of talent leads to a decline in productivity and innovation, hindering the country's ability to compete globally.

Additionally, brain drain exacerbates the economic disparity and inequality in Cuba. As the educated and skilled individuals emigrate, those left behind are often less educated and have limited access to opportunities. This further widens the gap between the haves and the have-nots, contributing to social unrest and economic instability.

Furthermore, the loss of human capital through brain drain hampers the development of critical sectors such as research and development. Without a strong pool of skilled professionals, Cuba is unable to invest in cutting-edge technologies and advancements, limiting its ability to attract foreign investment and compete in the global market.

To address the issue of brain drain, it is crucial for the Cuban government to implement policies that promote economic growth and provide opportunities for skilled professionals within the country. This includes investing in education and vocational training, creating a favorable business environment to attract foreign investment, and fostering innovation and entrepreneurship.

Moreover, it is essential to address the underlying causes of brain drain, such as limited access to technology, corruption, and economic mismanagement. By tackling these issues head-on, Cuba can create an environment that encourages talented individuals to stay and contribute to the country's development.

In conclusion, brain drain has had adverse implications for the Cuban economy, leading to a loss of human capital, limited innovation, and economic disparity. Addressing this issue requires a comprehensive approach that focuses on creating opportunities, improving governance, and investing in education and technology. Only then can Cuba unlock its full potential and overcome the challenges posed by brain drain.

Reasons for high emigration rates in Cuba

Introduction:

Cuba has experienced high emigration rates over the years, with a significant number of its citizens seeking opportunities abroad. While some may argue that the U.S. blockade is the primary cause of this phenomenon, a closer examination reveals that the reasons behind the high emigration rates lie in the mismanagement and incapacity of Cuban leaders. This subchapter aims to shed light on the various factors contributing to the emigration trend in Cuba, providing insights for scholars and economists interested in understanding the root causes of the issue.

1. Economic Mismanagement and Impact of Corruption:

Cuban leaders' mismanagement of the economy has resulted in widespread poverty, limited job prospects, and inadequate living conditions. Rampant corruption further exacerbates the situation, as it hinders economic development and perpetuates income inequality, prompting many to seek better opportunities elsewhere.

2. Inflation and Hyperinflation:

Cuba has been plagued by high inflation and occasional bouts of hyperinflation, eroding the purchasing power of its citizens. The resulting economic instability discourages investment and exacerbates poverty, leading to a desire among many to emigrate in search of a more stable economic environment.

3. Brain Drain and Economic Impact:

The emigration of highly skilled professionals from Cuba has had a detrimental impact on the economy. The loss of qualified doctors, engineers, and other professionals hinders the country's development and reduces its capacity to address critical societal needs.

4. Effects of Centralized Planning:

Cuba's centralized planning system, which concentrates decision-making power in the hands of a few, has stifled entrepreneurship and innovation. This lack of economic freedom and limited prospects for growth contribute to the desire to emigrate in search of greater opportunities.

5. Cuban Agriculture and Food Scarcity:

The mismanagement of the agricultural sector has led to chronic food scarcity in Cuba. Insufficient food production and distribution, coupled with import restrictions, have resulted in a lack of basic necessities. This economic hardship has prompted many Cubans to seek better living conditions elsewhere.

6. Economic Disparity and Inequality:

Cuba's socialist system has resulted in significant economic disparity, with a small elite enjoying privileges while the majority struggle to make ends meet. This inequality fuels resentment and frustration, driving many to seek a more equitable environment abroad.

7. Limited Foreign Investment:

Cuba's limited access to foreign investment and its failure to attract significant capital have hindered economic growth and job creation. The lack of opportunities and prospects for advancement further motivate individuals to emigrate in search of a better future.

8. Role of Black Market and Informal Economy:

The prevalence of a black market and informal economy in Cuba reflects the shortcomings of the formal economic system. Limited job opportunities and low wages have pushed many to engage in informal economic activities, contributing to the desire to emigrate in search of better income-generating opportunities.

9. Limited Access to Technology and Internet:

Cuba's restricted access to technology and the internet has hampered economic development and innovation. The lack of connectivity limits educational and professional opportunities, pushing many to seek access to these resources in other countries.

Conclusion:

While the U.S. blockade is often cited as the primary cause of high emigration rates in Cuba, a deeper analysis reveals that mismanagement, corruption, economic disparity, limited investment, and other internal factors play more significant roles. Understanding these root causes is crucial for scholars and economists interested in addressing the emigration issue and supporting sustainable economic development in Cuba.

Strategies to mitigate brain drain effects

The phenomenon of brain drain has had a significant impact on the Cuban economy, exacerbating the existing challenges faced by the country. However, there are strategies that can be implemented to mitigate these effects and foster economic growth. This subchapter explores some of the key strategies that can be adopted to address brain drain in Cuba.

1. Enhancing education and research: Investing in education and research is crucial to retain skilled professionals. By improving the quality of education and increasing funding for research institutions, Cuba can provide attractive opportunities for talented individuals, encouraging them to stay and contribute to the country's development.

2. Creating favorable working conditions: To retain skilled workers, it is essential to create a conducive environment that offers competitive salaries, career advancement opportunities, and a supportive work culture. This can be achieved by implementing policies that prioritize job satisfaction, work-life balance, and professional growth.

3. Encouraging entrepreneurship: Promoting entrepreneurship can help create job opportunities and retain skilled individuals who may otherwise seek opportunities abroad. By providing incentives and support for startups and small businesses, Cuba can stimulate economic growth and retain its human capital.

4. Strengthening healthcare and social services: Brain drain often affects the healthcare sector disproportionately. To mitigate this, Cuba can focus on improving healthcare infrastructure, providing better working conditions for medical professionals, and expanding access to quality healthcare services. Additionally, strengthening social services and welfare programs can help address some of the socio-economic challenges that contribute to brain drain.

5. Fostering international collaborations: Establishing partnerships with foreign institutions and organizations can facilitate knowledge exchange, collaboration, and capacity building. By encouraging international collaborations, Cuba can create opportunities for its professionals to gain exposure to global best practices while also attracting foreign expertise to contribute to the country's development.

6. Promoting return migration: Creating incentives for Cuban professionals who have emigrated to return to their home country can help counter brain drain. Offering attractive job prospects, access to research funding, and facilitating the reintegration process can encourage skilled individuals to come back and contribute to the country's progress.

7. Addressing political and economic challenges: Brain drain is often fueled by political and economic instability. Therefore, it is essential to address the root causes of these challenges. By promoting political stability, transparency, and economic reforms, Cuba can create an environment that encourages its skilled professionals to stay and contribute to the country's growth.

In conclusion, implementing these strategies can help mitigate the effects of brain drain in Cuba. By prioritizing education, creating favorable working conditions, fostering entrepreneurship, strengthening healthcare and social services, promoting international collaborations, encouraging return migration, and addressing political and economic challenges, Cuba can retain its human capital and foster sustainable economic development.

Chapter 7: Effects of Centralized Planning on Cuban Economy

Overview of centralized planning in Cuba

Centralized planning is a key feature of the Cuban economic system, where the government plays a central role in planning and directing economic activities. This subchapter will provide an overview of the concept of centralized planning in Cuba and its impact on the country's economy.

In Cuba, centralized planning is implemented through the National Economic Plan, which sets targets and priorities for various sectors of the economy. The plan is developed by the central planning authority, the Ministry of Economy and Planning, in consultation with other government bodies and economic enterprises. This top-down approach aims to coordinate and control economic activities to achieve desired social and economic outcomes.

One of the primary goals of centralized planning in Cuba is to ensure social equity and equal access to basic goods and services. The government heavily subsidizes basic necessities such as food, healthcare, and education, which are provided at low or no cost to the population. This has contributed to relatively high levels of social welfare and human development indicators in Cuba compared to other developing countries.

However, centralized planning has also led to several challenges and inefficiencies in the Cuban economy. One of the major issues is the lack of market mechanisms to allocate resources efficiently. The government's control over prices, production, and distribution often leads to shortages, inefficiencies, and low productivity. This has resulted in persistent food scarcity, limited consumer choices, and poor quality of goods and services.

Furthermore, centralized planning has hindered innovation and entrepreneurship in Cuba. The lack of economic freedom and limited opportunities for private enterprise have discouraged investment and stifled economic growth. The state-dominated economy has also resulted in a brain drain, as talented individuals seek better opportunities abroad, further exacerbating the country's economic challenges.

Moreover, the centralized planning model has contributed to economic disparity and inequality in Cuba. While basic goods and services are provided to all citizens, there are significant disparities in income and wealth distribution. The state sector, which dominates the economy, provides relatively low wages, while the emerging private sector offers higher income opportunities but is limited in scope and size.

In conclusion, centralized planning in Cuba has had both positive and negative impacts on the country's economy. While it has ensured social equity and basic welfare for the population, it has also led to inefficiencies, shortages, and limited economic opportunities. Moving forward, it is crucial for Cuba to strike a balance between centralized planning and market mechanisms to foster sustainable economic growth and prosperity for its citizens.

Shortcomings and limitations of centralized planning

Centralized planning, as implemented in Cuba, has had numerous shortcomings and limitations that have contributed to the economic misery experienced by the country. This subchapter delves into the key issues related to centralized planning and its impact on the Cuban economy.

One of the major problems with centralized planning is the lack of flexibility and adaptability. The central planning model, where decisions are made by a small group of government officials, often leads to a slow and inefficient decision-making process. This hampers the ability to respond quickly to changing economic conditions, resulting in missed opportunities and a failure to address emerging challenges.

Another significant limitation of centralized planning is the lack of incentives for innovation and entrepreneurship. When the government controls most economic activities, there is little room for individual initiative and market competition. This stifles creativity and discourages risk-taking, leading to a stagnant economy that struggles to keep up with global trends.

Centralized planning also contributes to the misallocation of resources. Without market forces guiding the allocation of resources, there is a tendency for inefficient use of available assets. Industries that are favored by the government may receive excessive resources, while others deemed less important are neglected. This leads to an imbalance in the economy and a misallocation of resources, resulting in inefficiency and reduced productivity.

Furthermore, centralized planning often fails to accurately assess consumer preferences and demand. The government's control over production and distribution means that it is the ultimate decision-maker in determining what goods and services are produced and made available to the public. However, this top-down approach neglects the diverse needs and preferences of consumers, resulting in a lack of variety and quality in the goods and services offered.

Additionally, centralized planning tends to discourage foreign investment. Investors are often deterred by the lack of transparency, bureaucratic hurdles, and limited economic freedoms associated with centralized planning. This leads to a reduced inflow of foreign capital, which is crucial for economic growth and development.

In conclusion, the shortcomings and limitations of centralized planning in Cuba have contributed significantly to the economic misery experienced by the country. The lack of flexibility, limited incentives for innovation, misallocation of resources, and failure to meet consumer demands are among the key issues. Addressing these limitations and transitioning towards a more market-oriented economy could help alleviate the economic challenges faced by Cuba and improve the standard of living for its citizens.

Alternative economic models for Cuba

Introduction:

Cuba has long been struggling with economic mismanagement and the consequences of centralized planning. The traditional economic model in Cuba has proven to be ineffective in addressing the country's economic challenges, resulting in high levels of poverty, inequality, and scarcity. This subchapter explores alternative economic models that could potentially alleviate Cuba's economic misery.

1. Market-oriented reforms:

One alternative economic model for Cuba could involve implementing market-oriented reforms. This approach would involve reducing government intervention in the economy and allowing market forces to play a more significant role. By encouraging private businesses, foreign investment, and competition, Cuba could stimulate economic growth, create job opportunities, and increase efficiency in various sectors.

2. Mixed economy:

Another alternative model is the adoption of a mixed economy, which combines both elements of socialism and capitalism. This approach would allow Cuba to maintain some degree of central planning while also allowing for private enterprise and market-driven activities. By embracing a mixed economy, Cuba could diversify its economic structure, encourage innovation, and create a more resilient and sustainable economy.

3. Sustainable agriculture:

Cuba's agriculture sector has been plagued by inefficiencies and food scarcity. An alternative economic model for Cuba could focus on sustainable agriculture practices, such as organic farming, agroecology, and small-scale farming cooperatives. By promoting these practices, Cuba could increase food production, reduce dependency on imports, and improve the overall quality of the agricultural sector.

4. Technological advancements:

Limited access to technology and the internet has hindered Cuba's economic development. An alternative economic model could prioritize technological advancements and digital infrastructure. By investing in technology and promoting internet access, Cuba could enhance productivity, innovation, and connectivity with the global economy.

Conclusion:

Cuba's economic misery is not solely due to the US blockade but is largely a result of mismanagement, corruption, and the limitations of a centrally planned economy. Exploring alternative economic models could provide valuable insights and potential solutions to Cuba's economic challenges. By considering market-oriented reforms, embracing a mixed economy, focusing on sustainable agriculture, and investing in technology, Cuba could pave the way for a more prosperous and equitable future. Scholars and economists should further study and discuss these alternative economic models to contribute to a comprehensive understanding of Cuba's economic situation and potential solutions for improvement.

Chapter 8: Cuban Agriculture and Food Scarcity

Challenges faced by the agricultural sector in Cuba

The agricultural sector in Cuba has long faced numerous challenges that have hindered its growth and development. These challenges are not solely due to the US blockade, as often claimed, but are also a result of mismanagement and incapacity by Cuban leaders. This subchapter aims to shed light on the various obstacles that have plagued the agricultural sector in Cuba.

One of the major challenges is the impact of corruption on the Cuban economy. Corruption has infiltrated all levels of the agricultural sector, from land distribution to supply chains and distribution networks. This has led to misallocation of resources, inefficiencies, and a lack of transparency, ultimately impeding the sector's productivity and growth.

Inflation and hyperinflation have also posed significant challenges to the agricultural sector. The fluctuating prices of inputs, such as fertilizers and machinery, have made it difficult for farmers to plan and invest in their operations. Moreover, hyperinflation has eroded the purchasing power of consumers, leading to a decrease in demand for agricultural products.

The economic impact of brain drain in Cuba has been detrimental to the agricultural sector as well. Many skilled workers, including agronomists and researchers, have left the country in search of better opportunities abroad. This brain drain has resulted in a loss of expertise and knowledge, hindering the sector's ability to innovate and adapt to new technologies and practices.

The effects of centralized planning on the Cuban economy have also had a negative impact on the agricultural sector. The top-down approach to decision-making has stifled entrepreneurship and limited the autonomy of farmers. This has resulted in a lack of incentive for productivity and innovation, leading to low agricultural output and food scarcity.

Furthermore, limited foreign investment in Cuba has constrained the growth of the agricultural sector. The government's strict regulations and restrictions on foreign ownership have deterred potential investors. This has resulted in a lack of capital and technology infusion, preventing the sector from modernizing and becoming more efficient.

The role of the black market and informal economy cannot be ignored when discussing the challenges faced by the agricultural sector. Due to limited access to formal markets and high prices, many farmers resort to selling their produce on the black market. This undermines the formal economy and perpetuates inefficiencies in the sector.

Limited access to technology and the internet has also hindered the agricultural sector's growth. The lack of modern farming techniques, information, and access to markets has limited farmers' ability to increase their productivity and reach wider consumer bases.

In conclusion, the challenges faced by the agricultural sector in Cuba are multi-faceted and cannot be solely attributed to the US blockade. Mismanagement, corruption, inflation, brain drain, centralized planning, limited foreign investment, the black market, and restricted access to technology and the internet all contribute to the sector's struggles. Addressing these challenges requires a comprehensive approach that includes structural reforms, increased transparency, and the promotion of innovation and investment. Only then can the agricultural sector in Cuba overcome its obstacles and contribute to the country's economic development.

Food scarcity and its impact on the population

Food scarcity is a critical issue that has plagued the Cuban population for decades. Despite being a country with fertile land and a favorable climate for agricultural production, the Cuban people have suffered from chronic shortages of basic food items. This subchapter aims to explore the causes and consequences of food scarcity in Cuba, shedding light on the complex dynamics that have led to this dire situation.

One of the primary reasons behind food scarcity in Cuba is the mismanagement and incapacity of its leaders. The Cuban government, under a centralized planning system, has failed to effectively allocate resources, implement efficient agricultural practices, and develop sustainable food production systems. The absence of competition and limited private enterprise in the agricultural sector has hindered innovation and productivity, resulting in a consistent lack of food supplies.

Moreover, corruption has deeply impacted the Cuban economy, exacerbating food scarcity. The diversion of resources and funds intended for agricultural development and food imports has deprived the population of the necessary sustenance. This corruption, coupled with limited foreign investment, has severely hampered the country's ability to modernize its agricultural practices and diversify its food production.

The economic consequences of limited access to technology and the internet have also played a significant role in exacerbating food scarcity in Cuba. The lack of technological advancements and digital infrastructure has hindered the dissemination of knowledge and hindered the adoption of efficient farming techniques. As a result, agricultural productivity has remained stagnant, perpetuating the cycle of food scarcity.

The impact of food scarcity on the Cuban population cannot be overstated. It has led to a rise in malnutrition rates, particularly among vulnerable groups such as children and the elderly. The lack of access to a balanced diet and essential nutrients has resulted in long-term health issues and hindered the overall development of the population.

Furthermore, the economic disparity and inequality prevalent in Cuba have exacerbated the effects of food scarcity. The limited availability of food has led to a thriving black market and informal economy, where the wealthy can obtain essential goods at exorbitant prices, further marginalizing the poor and widening the economic divide.

In conclusion, food scarcity in Cuba is not a result of the US blockade as often claimed by the Cuban government. Rather, it is primarily a consequence of mismanagement, corruption, limited access to technology, and an inefficient centralized planning system. The impact of food scarcity on the Cuban population is profound, perpetuating malnutrition and exacerbating economic inequality. Addressing these issues is crucial to ensure the well-being and sustainable development of the Cuban people.

Potential solutions to improve agricultural productivity

Agricultural productivity plays a crucial role in ensuring food security, economic development, and overall well-being in any country. In the case of Cuba, where agricultural productivity has been a persistent challenge, it is essential to explore potential solutions to address this issue. This subchapter aims to discuss some potential strategies that can be implemented to improve agricultural productivity in Cuba.

1. Modernization of agricultural practices: One key solution is to modernize agricultural practices by adopting advanced technologies, machinery, and equipment. This would help increase efficiency, reduce labor-intensive processes, and enhance overall productivity. Introducing precision agriculture techniques, such as the use of drones and satellite imagery, can also improve crop management and yield.

2. Investment in research and development: Allocating resources to agricultural research and development can lead to the development of new crop varieties, improved farming techniques, and better pest and disease management strategies. Collaborations with international research institutions can bring in expertise and knowledge exchange, accelerating agricultural innovation.

3. Promotion of sustainable farming practices: Encouraging the adoption of sustainable farming practices, such as organic farming, agroecology, and permaculture, can have multiple benefits. These practices help conserve natural resources, reduce reliance on chemical inputs, and enhance soil fertility, ultimately leading to increased agricultural productivity in the long run.

4. Support for small-scale farmers: Recognizing the crucial role played by small-scale farmers, it is important to provide them with necessary support and resources. This can include access to credit facilities, training programs, extension services, and improved infrastructure. Creating farmer cooperatives can also enhance their bargaining power and help them access larger markets.

5. Strengthening agricultural education and extension services: Investing in agricultural education, research institutions, and extension services can enhance the knowledge and skills of farmers. This would enable them to adopt best practices, improve their decision-making abilities, and effectively manage their farms.

6. Enhancing market access and value chains: Improving market access for farmers and strengthening agricultural value chains can ensure fair prices and reduce post-harvest losses. Developing storage and processing facilities, improving transportation infrastructure, and promoting farmer-producer partnerships can help connect farmers directly with consumers and reduce dependency on intermediaries.

In conclusion, improving agricultural productivity in Cuba requires a multi-faceted approach. By modernizing practices, investing in research and development, promoting sustainability, supporting small-scale farmers, strengthening education and extension services, and enhancing market access, Cuba can address its agricultural challenges and move towards a more prosperous and food-secure future.

Chapter 9: Economic Disparity and Inequality in Cuba

Income inequality in Cuba

Income inequality in Cuba has been a persistent issue that has plagued the country for decades. Despite the Cuban government's claims of achieving a more egalitarian society through socialist policies, the reality is quite different. This subchapter aims to explore the various facets of income inequality in Cuba, shedding light on the factors that contribute to this disparity and debunking the popular notion that the US blockade is solely responsible for the country's economic misery.

One of the key factors contributing to income inequality in Cuba is the mismanagement and incapacity of its leaders. The Cuban government's centralized planning and control over the economy have stifled innovation and entrepreneurship, resulting in a limited number of opportunities for economic advancement. This has led to a situation where a small elite class, which includes government officials and their associates, enjoys significant privileges and access to resources, while the majority of the population struggles to make ends meet.

Corruption is another major factor that exacerbates income inequality in Cuba. The lack of transparency and accountability in the government has created an environment where bribery and embezzlement are rampant. This further concentrates wealth in the hands of a few, while ordinary citizens suffer the consequences of a deteriorating economy.

Inflation and hyperinflation have also played a significant role in widening the income gap in Cuba. The government's excessive money printing and price controls have led to a situation where the cost of basic goods and services far exceeds the purchasing power of the average

Cuban. This disproportionately affects the lower-income segments of society, pushing them further into poverty.

The brain drain phenomenon has had a profound economic impact on Cuba. The emigration of highly skilled professionals and intellectuals seeking better opportunities abroad has resulted in a significant loss of human capital. This brain drain has further limited the country's capacity for economic growth and perpetuated the cycle of income inequality.

Limited foreign investment in Cuba has also contributed to the economic disparity in the country. The government's strict regulations and restrictions on foreign businesses have deterred potential investors, leaving the economy heavily reliant on a few key sectors such as tourism. This concentration of foreign investment exacerbates income inequality, as the benefits are mostly reaped by the privileged few.

Overall, income inequality in Cuba is a multifaceted issue that cannot be solely attributed to the US blockade. The mismanagement and incapacity of the Cuban leaders, corruption, inflation, brain drain, limited foreign investment, and the impact of centralized planning all play significant roles in perpetuating economic disparity. By understanding these factors, scholars and economists can gain a more nuanced perspective on the root causes of income inequality in Cuba and work towards finding sustainable solutions for a more equitable society.

Social and economic consequences of economic disparity

Economic disparity is a pressing issue in Cuba, with profound social and economic consequences that have far-reaching implications. This subchapter sheds light on the various facets of this issue and explores its impact on the Cuban society and economy.

One significant factor contributing to economic disparity in Cuba is the mismanagement and incapacity of the country's leaders. Despite the prevailing narrative that blames the US blockage for Cuba's economic misery, it is the internal mismanagement that has led to a deteriorating economy. Scholars and economists must critically analyze the policies and decision-making of the Cuban government to understand the root causes of economic disparity.

Corruption also plays a substantial role in exacerbating economic disparity in Cuba. The diversion of resources and funds intended for public welfare into the hands of corrupt officials further widens the gap between the rich and the poor. Scholars and economists must explore the impact of corruption on the Cuban economy to devise effective strategies for combating this issue.

Inflation and hyperinflation have plagued the Cuban economy, leading to increased economic disparity. The rising costs of goods and services disproportionately affect the lower-income segments of society, pushing them further into poverty. Scholars and economists must investigate the causes of inflation and hyperinflation in Cuba to propose measures for stabilizing the economy and alleviating economic disparity.

Brain drain, the emigration of skilled individuals, has a detrimental impact on the Cuban economy. The loss of human capital weakens the labor force and hinders economic growth, perpetuating economic disparity. Scholars and economists should analyze the economic impact of brain drain in Cuba and explore ways to retain and utilize the country's talent for its development.

The effects of centralized planning on the Cuban economy cannot be overlooked. The lack of market mechanisms and private enterprise stifles innovation and hampers economic growth, resulting in increased economic disparity. Scholars and economists must examine the consequences of centralized planning and advocate for reforms that foster a more inclusive and dynamic economy.

Cuban agriculture and food scarcity are intimately linked to economic disparity. Limited access to resources, outdated farming techniques, and government control over the sector have led to food shortages and unequal distribution. Scholars and economists must explore strategies to enhance agricultural productivity and address food scarcity, thereby reducing economic disparity.

Limited foreign investment in Cuba has had a detrimental economic impact, exacerbating economic disparity. The lack of capital and technology inflow hinders economic development and perpetuates income inequality. Scholars and economists should analyze the consequences of limited foreign investment and propose measures to attract investment and foster economic growth.

The black market and informal economy also contribute to economic disparity in Cuba. Scholars and economists must examine the role of these sectors in the economy and explore ways to integrate them into the formal economy, ensuring fair opportunities for all segments of society.

Lastly, limited access to technology and the internet widens the digital divide and deepens economic disparity in Cuba. Scholars and economists must investigate the economic consequences of limited access to technology and propose strategies to bridge the digital gap, fostering inclusive economic growth.

In conclusion, economic disparity in Cuba has profound social and economic consequences. Scholars and economists have a crucial role in debunking the myth of the US blockage and shedding light on the internal mismanagement and incapacity of Cuban leaders as the true culprits behind the country's economic misery. By analyzing the impact of corruption, inflation, brain drain, centralized planning, limited foreign investment, the black market, and limited access to technology, scholars and economists can offer valuable insights and propose effective solutions to reduce economic disparity and foster a more equitable and prosperous Cuba.

Policies to reduce inequality in Cuba

Introduction:

In Cuba, the issue of economic disparity and inequality has been a persistent challenge, impacting various aspects of the nation's economy and society. To address this issue, it is crucial for policymakers to implement effective policies aimed at reducing inequality and promoting economic prosperity for all citizens. This subchapter explores potential policies that can be pursued to tackle inequality in Cuba, focusing on areas such as education, healthcare, social welfare, and economic reforms.

Education Reforms:

One key policy to reduce inequality is to prioritize education and invest in improving the quality and accessibility of education across the country. This can be accomplished by enhancing teacher training programs, modernizing educational infrastructure, and expanding access to higher education institutions. Additionally, scholarships and financial aid should be provided to disadvantaged students to ensure equal opportunities for all.

Healthcare Reforms:

To address the disparities in healthcare access, policies should be implemented to improve the quality and availability of medical services throughout the country. This can involve increasing the number of medical professionals, enhancing healthcare infrastructure, and prioritizing preventive healthcare measures. Additionally, the government should ensure that healthcare services are affordable and accessible to all citizens, regardless of their socio-economic background.

Social Welfare Programs:

Implementing comprehensive social welfare programs can play a significant role in reducing inequality. These programs should focus on providing assistance to vulnerable groups such as the elderly, children, and individuals with disabilities. By ensuring a basic standard of living for all citizens, these programs can help alleviate poverty and inequality in Cuba.

Economic Reforms:

Promoting economic reforms is crucial to reducing inequality in Cuba. This can involve encouraging entrepreneurship, attracting foreign direct investment, and promoting small and medium-sized enterprises. By diversifying the economy and creating more job opportunities, these reforms can help reduce income disparities and promote economic growth.

Conclusion:

Reducing inequality in Cuba requires a comprehensive approach that addresses various aspects of the economy and society. By implementing policies that focus on education, healthcare, social welfare, and economic reforms, the Cuban government can make significant strides in reducing inequality and improving the overall well-being of its citizens. It is crucial for scholars and economists to analyze and support these policies to ensure their effectiveness and long-term impact on Cuba's economic prosperity.

Chapter 10: Economic Impact of Limited Foreign Investment in Cuba

Foreign investment policies in Cuba

Foreign investment policies in Cuba have played a significant role in the country's economic struggles. In order to understand the root causes of Cuban economic misery, it is crucial to examine the impact of these policies and how they have hindered the country's growth.

Cuba's foreign investment policies have traditionally been restrictive and highly regulated. This has deterred potential investors from entering the market, limiting the inflow of much-needed capital and expertise. The Cuban government has maintained a monopoly over key industries, making it difficult for foreign investors to participate in the country's economic development.

Furthermore, the lack of legal protection for foreign investors has been a major deterrent. The Cuban government has a history of expropriating foreign assets without adequate compensation, creating a climate of uncertainty and discouraging long-term investment. This lack of protection has made foreign investors reluctant to invest in Cuba, further stifling economic growth.

The limited foreign investment in Cuba has had severe economic consequences. The country's infrastructure is in a dire state, with crumbling roads, outdated factories, and inadequate public services. Foreign investment could have helped modernize these sectors and improve the overall productivity of the economy.

Additionally, limited foreign investment has resulted in a lack of technological advancements in Cuba. The country has struggled to keep up with global technological advancements, which has hindered its competitiveness in the global market. The absence of foreign investment has left the Cuban economy isolated and disconnected from the advancements in technology and innovation happening elsewhere in the world.

Moreover, the limited access to foreign investment has contributed to the economic disparity and inequality in Cuba. The lack of economic opportunities has led to a brain drain, with highly skilled professionals leaving the country in search of better prospects abroad. This brain drain further exacerbates the economic challenges faced by Cuba, as the country loses valuable human capital that could have contributed to its development.

In conclusion, the restrictive foreign investment policies in Cuba have had a detrimental impact on the country's economy. The limited inflow of capital, expertise, and technological advancements has hindered the country's growth and perpetuated economic misery. It is imperative for the Cuban government to reconsider its foreign investment policies and create a more welcoming environment for foreign investors in order to stimulate economic development and alleviate the economic challenges faced by the country.

Barriers and challenges faced by foreign investors

Subchapter: Barriers and Challenges Faced by Foreign Investors

Foreign investment plays a crucial role in the economic development of any country. However, in the case of Cuba, there are numerous barriers and challenges that foreign investors have to face. These challenges not only hinder the growth of the Cuban economy but also discourage potential investors from entering the market.

One of the major barriers faced by foreign investors in Cuba is the impact of corruption on the economy. Corruption is deeply entrenched in the Cuban system, and it poses a significant risk for foreign investors.

Bribery, nepotism, and lack of transparency in business transactions create an unfavorable environment for investment. This deters potential investors who seek stability and fair business practices.

Inflation and hyperinflation are other significant challenges faced by foreign investors in Cuba. The country has a history of unstable prices, which erodes the value of investments and raises the cost of doing business. This volatility makes it difficult for foreign investors to plan and allocate resources effectively.

The economic impact of brain drain is another hurdle for foreign investors in Cuba. The country has experienced a significant loss of skilled professionals who have emigrated in search of better opportunities. This brain drain has resulted in a shortage of skilled labor, hindering foreign investors who rely on a skilled workforce to operate efficiently.

Centralized planning in Cuba has also had adverse effects on the economy and foreign investment. The government's control over key sectors and industries restricts the autonomy of foreign investors. Lack of flexibility and bureaucratic red tape make it challenging to navigate the Cuban market, discouraging potential investors.

Cuban agriculture and food scarcity pose another challenge for foreign investors. The country heavily relies on imports to meet its food demands, which makes it vulnerable to fluctuations in global food prices. This volatility affects the profitability and sustainability of agricultural investments in Cuba.

Economic disparity and inequality in Cuba also act as barriers for foreign investors. The wide income gap and unequal distribution of wealth create social tensions, which can impact the stability of investments. Moreover, limited access to technology and the internet restricts the flow of information and hampers innovation, further deterring foreign investors who seek modern infrastructure and connectivity.

Lastly, the role of the black market and informal economy in Cuba cannot be overlooked. These unregulated sectors undermine the formal economy, creating unfair competition for foreign investors who operate within legal frameworks.

In conclusion, the barriers and challenges faced by foreign investors in Cuba are multi-faceted and interconnected. Corruption, inflation, brain drain, centralized planning, agricultural issues, economic disparity, limited foreign investment, the black market, and limited access to technology all contribute to creating an unfavorable investment climate. Addressing these challenges requires comprehensive reforms and a concerted effort from the Cuban government to create a more attractive and conducive environment for foreign investors.

Potential benefits of increased foreign investment

Subchapter: Potential Benefits of Increased Foreign Investment

Introduction:

Foreign investment has the potential to play a crucial role in alleviating the economic misery faced by Cuba. This subchapter explores the potential benefits that could arise from increased foreign investment in the country. By attracting foreign capital, Cuba can stimulate economic growth, create employment opportunities, enhance productivity, and diversify its economy. This chapter aims to shed light on the positive impact that foreign investment could have on various aspects of the Cuban economy.

1. Economic Growth and Development:

Increased foreign investment can act as a catalyst for economic growth in Cuba. By injecting capital into key sectors such as manufacturing, tourism, and infrastructure, foreign investors can contribute to the expansion of industries and the overall GDP. This, in turn, can lead to job creation, increased wages, and improved living standards for the Cuban population.

2. Technological Advancement:

Foreign investment brings with it new technologies, knowledge, and expertise that can benefit the Cuban economy. By collaborating with foreign investors, Cuba can gain access to advanced production techniques, management practices, and innovation. This exchange of knowledge can result in increased productivity, improved efficiency, and the development of new industries.

3. Diversification of the Economy:

Cuba has traditionally relied heavily on a few key sectors, such as agriculture and tourism. Increased foreign investment can help diversify the economy by attracting investors to other sectors such as manufacturing, renewable energy, and information technology. This diversification can reduce the country's vulnerability to external shocks and create a more resilient and sustainable economy.

4. Job Creation and Skills Development:

Foreign investment can contribute significantly to employment generation in Cuba. As foreign companies establish operations or expand existing ones, they create job opportunities for the local workforce. This not only reduces unemployment but also provides avenues for skills development and technology transfer, enhancing the human capital of the country.

5. Infrastructure Development:

Foreign investment can play a vital role in improving Cuba's infrastructure, which is crucial for economic development. By investing in transportation, energy, telecommunications, and other critical infrastructure projects, foreign investors can enhance the country's connectivity and productivity. This, in turn, can attract more investment and stimulate further economic growth.

Conclusion:

Increased foreign investment has the potential to bring about several positive changes to the Cuban economy. From fostering economic growth and diversification to creating employment opportunities and enhancing infrastructure, the benefits of attracting foreign capital are significant. By understanding and addressing the underlying challenges, Cuba can effectively harness the potential benefits of increased foreign investment and move towards a path of economic prosperity and development.

Chapter 11: Role of Black Market and Informal Economy in Cuba

Black market activities in Cuba

Black market activities in Cuba have played a significant role in the country's economy, impacting various sectors and exacerbating the existing economic misery. This subchapter aims to shed light on the prevalence and consequences of these activities, emphasizing that the US blockade is not solely responsible for Cuba's economic woes.

The black market in Cuba is a result of the government's centralized planning and limited access to resources. With limited foreign investment and a stagnant economy, many Cubans turn to underground markets to meet their basic needs. The black market offers goods and services that are scarce or unavailable in the state-controlled economy, ranging from food and household items to clothing and electronics.

One of the main reasons for the growth of the black market is the impact of corruption on the Cuban economy. Government officials and state employees often engage in illegal activities, such as embezzlement and bribery, to supplement their meager incomes. This corruption further exacerbates economic disparities and undermines the government's efforts to address economic issues.

Inflation and hyperinflation also contribute to the expansion of the black market. The Cuban government's mismanagement of the economy and excessive printing of money have led to a devaluation of the national currency. As prices skyrocket, many Cubans resort to the black market, where prices may be lower and goods more readily available.

Furthermore, the brain drain in Cuba has had a detrimental economic impact. Highly skilled professionals, disillusioned by limited opportunities and low wages, seek better prospects abroad. This brain drain not only deprives the country of valuable human capital but also hampers economic development and innovation, perpetuating the cycle of economic misery.

The role of the black market and the informal economy cannot be underestimated in Cuba. These activities provide an essential lifeline for many Cubans, enabling them to access goods and services that are otherwise out of reach. However, they also perpetuate economic inequality and hinder the government's attempts to implement effective economic policies.

In conclusion, the black market activities in Cuba are a symptom of the country's economic mismanagement, corruption, brain drain, and limited access to resources. While the US blockade may have some impact, it is crucial to recognize that the root causes of Cuba's economic misery lie within the country itself. Addressing these issues requires comprehensive reforms, transparency, and effective governance to create a more prosperous and equitable future for all Cubans.

Informal economy and its significance

Informal economy refers to economic activities that are not regulated or monitored by the government, and thus, are not included in the official calculations of a country's GDP. In the case of Cuba, the informal economy plays a significant role in the country's economic landscape and has important implications for its citizens.

The significance of the informal economy in Cuba cannot be overlooked. With limited opportunities for formal employment and a centrally planned economic system, many Cubans turn to the informal sector as a means of survival. This sector includes activities such as small-scale entrepreneurship, street vending, and unregistered self-employment.

One of the key reasons for the prevalence of the informal economy in Cuba is the impact of the US blockade. The embargo has limited access to foreign investment, technology, and resources, making it difficult for the formal economy to thrive. As a result, many Cubans have resorted to informal activities to make a living and meet their basic needs.

The informal economy also plays a crucial role in mitigating the impact of corruption on the Cuban economy. With pervasive corruption at various levels of government, formal sector businesses often face numerous bureaucratic obstacles and demands for bribes. In contrast, the informal sector allows individuals to operate outside of these corrupt systems and engage in economic activities with greater freedom and efficiency.

Moreover, the informal economy helps alleviate the consequences of economic disparity and inequality in Cuba. With limited access to resources and opportunities, marginalized communities often rely on the informal sector to generate income and improve their livelihoods. This informal sector serves as a safety net for those who have been left behind by the formal economy.

The role of the informal economy in Cuba also extends to addressing the issue of limited foreign investment. As foreign investment remains restricted, the informal sector becomes a vital source of entrepreneurship and innovation. It allows individuals to create their own businesses and contribute to the local economy, despite the obstacles posed by limited access to capital and resources.

In conclusion, the informal economy in Cuba is of significant importance. It serves as a means of survival for many Cubans, mitigates the impact of corruption, helps address economic disparity and inequality, and provides a source of entrepreneurship in the face of limited foreign investment. Recognizing the significance of the informal economy is crucial for understanding the complexities of Cuba's economic situation and exploring potential avenues for development and improvement.

Implications for the formal economy and government policies

The Cuban economy has long been mired in economic misery, and it is time to debunk the myth that the United States' blockade is solely responsible for this state of affairs. This subchapter delves into the implications for the formal economy and government policies in Cuba, shedding light on the real causes behind the country's economic woes.

One of the most pressing issues affecting the Cuban economy is the impact of corruption. Rampant corruption within the government and state-owned enterprises has hindered economic growth, eroded public trust, and deterred foreign investment. Scholars and economists must explore strategies to combat corruption and promote transparency to create a conducive environment for economic prosperity.

Inflation and hyperinflation have also plagued the Cuban economy, making it increasingly difficult for citizens to afford basic necessities. Government policies that consistently overspend and print money without proper fiscal control have contributed to this economic instability. Scholars and economists must analyze these policies and propose solutions to curb inflationary pressures and stabilize prices.

Brain drain, the emigration of skilled individuals, has had a profound economic impact on Cuba. The loss of talented professionals, particularly in sectors such as healthcare and engineering, has created a significant skills gap and hindered economic development. Scholars and economists should explore ways to incentivize skilled individuals to stay in Cuba and contribute to its economic growth.

Cuba's centralized planning model has also had adverse effects on its economy. The lack of market mechanisms and entrepreneurial freedom has stifled innovation and hindered productivity. Scholars and economists must evaluate alternative economic models that can foster competition, entrepreneurship, and efficiency in the Cuban economy.

The subchapter also delves into the issue of Cuban agriculture and food scarcity. Inefficiencies in the state-run agricultural sector, coupled with limited access to modern farming techniques and inputs, have resulted in insufficient food production. Scholars and economists should explore strategies to modernize the agricultural sector and boost food self-sufficiency.

Economic disparity and inequality in Cuba are also major concerns. The government's socialist policies have failed to bridge the wealth gap, leading to social unrest and discontent among citizens. Scholars and economists must analyze the root causes of economic disparity and propose policies that promote inclusive growth and equitable wealth distribution.

Limited foreign investment in Cuba has hindered its economic potential. Government policies that restrict foreign ownership and investment have deterred international businesses from entering the Cuban market. Scholars and economists should explore ways to attract foreign investment and foster economic cooperation with other countries.

The subchapter also highlights the role of the black market and informal economy in Cuba. These sectors have thrived due to restrictive government policies and limited formal employment opportunities. Scholars and economists should study the informal economy's impact on the formal sector and propose policies that can integrate informal workers into the formal economy.

Lastly, limited access to technology and the internet has had severe economic consequences in Cuba. The government's control over information flow and technological infrastructure has hindered innovation, productivity, and connectivity with the global economy. Scholars and economists must explore strategies to expand access to technology and the internet, fostering economic growth and integration.

In conclusion, understanding the implications for the formal economy and government policies in Cuba is crucial for scholars and economists aiming to debunk the myth of the US blockade's sole responsibility for the country's economic misery. By addressing issues such as corruption, inflation, brain drain, centralized planning, agriculture, economic disparity, foreign investment, the black market, and limited access to technology, scholars and economists can contribute to the discourse on Cuba's economic challenges and propose viable solutions for a brighter future.

Chapter 12: Economic Consequences of Limited Access to Technology and Internet in Cuba

Overview of technology and internet restrictions in Cuba

Cuba, a Caribbean island nation, has been subject to strict technology and internet restrictions for decades. These restrictions have had a significant impact on the country's economy, society, and the daily lives of its citizens. Understanding the nature and consequences of these restrictions is essential for scholars and economists studying the Cuban economy and its challenges.

Under the leadership of the Cuban government, technology and internet access have been tightly controlled and limited. The government has maintained a monopoly on telecommunications, with the state-run company ETECSA being the sole provider of internet services. This monopoly has resulted in high prices, slow speeds, and limited access for the majority of the population.

Internet connectivity in Cuba is one of the lowest in the world, with only a small percentage of the population having access. This limited access hampers communication, hinders the exchange of information, and inhibits economic development. Scholars and economists studying the impact of limited access to technology and the internet in Cuba recognize that these restrictions have contributed to the country's economic misery.

The Cuban government justifies these restrictions by citing concerns about national security and the preservation of the socialist system. However, critics argue that these restrictions are primarily aimed at controlling information and stifling dissent. The government heavily censors online content, blocking access to websites critical of the regime and filtering out information that does not align with their ideology.

The consequences of these restrictions are far-reaching. They hinder innovation, impede the growth of the private sector, and discourage foreign investment. Limited access to technology and the internet also exacerbates inequality, as those with connections and resources can circumvent the restrictions while the majority of the population is left behind.

To address the economic challenges faced by Cuba, it is crucial to acknowledge and analyze the impact of limited access to technology and the internet. Scholars and economists must consider how these restrictions contribute to the country's economic misery, hinder development, and perpetuate inequality. By understanding the nature and consequences of these restrictions, policymakers and researchers can work towards finding solutions that promote economic growth, innovation, and greater access to technology and the internet for all Cubans.

Economic effects of limited access to technology

In the modern world, access to technology and the internet has become increasingly essential for economic growth and development. However, in the case of Cuba, limited access to technology has had significant economic consequences. This subchapter aims to shed light on the economic effects of limited access to technology in Cuba and debunk the myth that the US blockade is solely responsible for Cuba's economic misery.

Firstly, limited access to technology hampers innovation and productivity. Without the latest technological advancements, Cuban industries struggle to compete globally and remain stagnant. This lack of competitiveness leads to a decline in exports and foreign investment, further exacerbating Cuba's economic woes.

Additionally, limited access to technology stifles entrepreneurship and small business growth. Start-ups and small businesses heavily rely on technology to streamline operations, reach new markets, and connect with customers. The absence of these technological tools hinders the growth potential of Cuban businesses, limiting job creation and economic diversification.

Moreover, the limited availability of technology directly impacts education and human capital development. Access to the internet and digital resources is crucial for quality education and skill-building. Without these resources, Cuban students and professionals are at a disadvantage, hindering their ability to compete in the global job market. This brain drain and lack of skilled workers further contribute to Cuba's economic struggles.

Furthermore, limited access to technology hampers information flow and transparency, leading to increased corruption. In a technologically advanced world, access to information is key to holding public officials accountable and ensuring efficient governance. However, without proper access to technology, Cuba's government faces challenges in implementing transparent policies and combating corruption effectively.

Lastly, limited access to technology also affects healthcare and public services in Cuba. Advanced medical technologies and digital health systems play a crucial role in providing quality healthcare. Without access to these technologies, Cuban citizens are deprived of essential medical advancements, resulting in a decline in healthcare standards and overall well-being.

In conclusion, limited access to technology in Cuba has had significant economic consequences. While the US blockade is often blamed for

Cuba's economic misery, this subchapter aims to debunk the myth and highlight the role of limited access to technology in perpetuating Cuba's economic struggles. It is crucial for scholars, economists, and policymakers to recognize the importance of addressing this issue and finding solutions to bridge the technology gap in order to promote economic growth and development in Cuba.

Strategies to promote technological advancement in Cuba

Introduction:

Technological advancement has become a critical factor in driving economic growth and development worldwide. However, Cuba has faced significant challenges in this area due to limited access to technology and the internet, which has hindered its progress. In this subchapter, we will explore strategies that can be employed to promote technological advancement in Cuba, ultimately contributing to the overall economic growth and development of the country.

Investment in Research and Development:

One of the key strategies to promote technological advancement in Cuba is to increase investment in research and development (R&D). Allocating more resources towards scientific research and innovation will foster the creation of new technologies and enhance the country's capacity to develop and adapt existing ones. By establishing partnerships with international research institutions, Cuba can tap into global knowledge networks and benefit from collaborative efforts to address its technological gaps.

Promotion of STEM Education:

A strong emphasis on science, technology, engineering, and mathematics (STEM) education is crucial to cultivating a skilled workforce capable of driving technological advancement. Cuba should invest in revamping its education system to prioritize STEM subjects from primary to tertiary levels. By encouraging more students to pursue careers in technology-related fields, the country can create a talent pool that will enhance its innovative capacity.

Encouraging Foreign Direct Investment:

Another effective strategy is to attract foreign direct investment (FDI) in the technology sector. By offering incentives such as tax breaks, streamlined regulations, and access to specialized infrastructure, Cuba can attract foreign companies seeking to expand their operations. This influx of FDI will not only bring much-needed capital but also transfer technology and knowledge, fostering a spillover effect that can benefit domestic industries and promote technological advancements.

Strengthening Intellectual Property Rights:

To encourage innovation and technological progress, Cuba needs to strengthen its intellectual property rights (IPR) framework. By implementing comprehensive IPR laws and regulations, the country can protect the rights of innovators and incentivize them to invest in research and development. This will create a favorable environment for technological advancements, as inventors will have confidence that their intellectual property is protected.

Promoting Public-Private Partnerships:

Encouraging collaboration between the public and private sectors is vital for technological advancement. By fostering public-private partnerships, Cuba can leverage the expertise and resources of both sectors to drive innovation and technology transfer. This collaboration can lead to the development of new technologies and the adaptation of existing ones to address the specific needs of the country.

Conclusion:

Technological advancement is a critical driver of economic growth and development. By implementing strategies such as increasing investment in research and development, promoting STEM education, attracting foreign direct investment, strengthening intellectual property rights, and fostering public-private partnerships, Cuba can overcome its technological challenges and pave the way for a more prosperous and innovative future. These strategies, when implemented effectively, will not only contribute to the growth of Cuba's economy but also improve the overall well-being of its citizens.

Chapter 13: Conclusion

Summary of key findings

In the book "Cuban Economic Misery: Debunking the US Blockage Myth," a comprehensive analysis was conducted to investigate the root causes of Cuba's economic woes. This subchapter aims to provide scholars and economists with a summary of the key findings uncovered throughout the research. By examining various aspects such as corruption, inflation, brain drain, centralized planning, agriculture, economic disparity, limited foreign investment, the black market, and limited access to technology, a clearer picture emerges.

Firstly, it is evident that Cuban economic misery cannot be solely attributed to the US blockade. While the blockade has undoubtedly had an impact, the mismanagement and incapacity of Cuban leaders have played a significant role in exacerbating the situation. This finding challenges the widely held belief that the US blockade is the primary cause of Cuba's economic struggles.

Secondly, corruption has severely hampered the Cuban economy. The prevalence of corruption within the government and various institutions has led to a misallocation of resources, hindering economic growth and exacerbating poverty. Addressing this issue is crucial for any meaningful economic reform in Cuba.

Furthermore, the research highlights the detrimental effects of inflation and hyperinflation on the Cuban economy. The continuous devaluation of the Cuban peso has eroded purchasing power, leading to decreased standards of living for the population. Efforts to stabilize the currency and control inflation are imperative for economic recovery.

The brain drain phenomena have also taken a toll on Cuba's economic development. The exodus of skilled professionals and intellectuals has left a void in crucial sectors, impacting innovation, productivity, and overall economic growth. Strategies to attract and retain talent are necessary to reverse this brain drain trend.

Centralized planning, a hallmark of the Cuban economic system, has proven to be detrimental. The lack of market mechanisms, flexibility, and incentives has stifled productivity and innovation, hindering economic progress. Reforms that promote decentralization and market-oriented policies could stimulate growth and improve living conditions.

The state of Cuban agriculture and food scarcity is another critical concern. The inefficiencies and bureaucratic obstacles within the agricultural sector have resulted in insufficient food production and distribution. Addressing these issues through market-oriented reforms and increased investment in agriculture is crucial to alleviate food scarcity.

Economic disparity and inequality within Cuba have been increasingly pronounced. The unequal distribution of wealth and opportunities has created social unrest and hindered economic progress. Policies aimed at reducing inequality and promoting social mobility are necessary for long-term economic stability.

Limited foreign investment in Cuba has had a significant impact on the economy. The absence of foreign capital and expertise has hindered growth, industrial development, and technological advancement. Encouraging foreign investment through policy reforms and creating an attractive business environment is essential for economic rejuvenation.

The role of the black market and informal economy in Cuba cannot be overlooked. The prevalence of these underground activities has both positive and negative implications for the economy. Understanding the dynamics and finding ways to formalize and regulate these sectors could contribute to economic growth and stability.

Lastly, the limited access to technology and the internet has hampered Cuba's economic potential. The lack of connectivity and technological infrastructure has hindered innovation, productivity, and participation in the global economy. Expanding access to technology and the internet is crucial for economic development.

In conclusion, this subchapter highlights the key findings from the book "Cuban Economic Misery: Debunking the US Blockage Myth." It emphasizes that Cuba's economic challenges stem from a combination of factors, including mismanagement, corruption, brain drain, centralized planning, agricultural inefficiencies, economic disparity, limited foreign investment, the black market, and limited access to technology. Understanding these factors is essential for scholars, economists, and policymakers seeking to address Cuba's economic struggles and promote sustainable development.

Policy recommendations

In light of the various challenges faced by the Cuban economy, it is crucial to consider a range of policy recommendations that can help alleviate the economic misery experienced by the Cuban people. This subchapter will outline several key policy recommendations, addressing issues such as the impact of corruption, inflation, brain drain, centralized planning, agriculture, economic disparity, limited foreign investment, the black market, and limited access to technology and the internet.

Firstly, tackling corruption should be a priority for the Cuban government. Implementing comprehensive anti-corruption measures, such as strengthening transparency and accountability mechanisms, will help restore trust in the economy and attract both domestic and foreign investments.

Addressing inflation and hyperinflation requires implementing effective monetary policies. The government should focus on maintaining price stability, controlling excessive money supply, and reducing fiscal deficits. This will help prevent further erosion of purchasing power and ensure a more stable economic environment.

To mitigate the economic impact of brain drain, Cuba should create incentives for skilled professionals to remain in the country. Offering competitive wages, improving working conditions, and providing opportunities for professional growth can help retain talented individuals and prevent the loss of human capital.

The effects of centralized planning on the Cuban economy can be reduced by transitioning towards a more market-oriented system. Allowing greater participation of private enterprises, reducing state control, and creating an enabling environment for entrepreneurship can foster innovation and economic growth.

Improving the agricultural sector is crucial to addressing food scarcity. The government should implement policies that promote investment in agriculture, provide farmers with access to modern technology and resources, and incentivize increased productivity. Strengthening domestic food production will reduce reliance on imports and enhance food security.

To address economic disparity and inequality, the government should implement policies that promote equal opportunities for all citizens. This includes investing in education and healthcare, providing social safety nets, and promoting inclusive growth.

To attract foreign investment, Cuba should create a favorable business environment by implementing transparent and stable regulations, reducing bureaucratic barriers, and offering incentives to foreign investors. This will help diversify the economy, create jobs, and stimulate economic growth.

Recognizing the role of the black market and informal economy, the government should strive to formalize these sectors by reducing regulations and taxes. This will help bring these activities into the formal economy, enhancing tax revenues and promoting economic development.

Finally, expanding access to technology and the internet is crucial for economic growth. The government should invest in infrastructure, improve connectivity, and promote digital literacy. This will enable Cubans to access global markets, enhance productivity, and foster innovation.

In conclusion, addressing the economic misery in Cuba requires a comprehensive set of policy recommendations. By addressing corruption, inflation, brain drain, centralized planning, agriculture, economic disparity, limited foreign investment, the black market, and limited access to technology, the Cuban government can create an enabling environment for sustainable economic growth and improve the lives of its citizens.

Future research directions

While this book has aimed to debunk the myth that the US blockage is the primary cause of Cuban economic misery, there are still numerous research areas that require further exploration. Scholars and economists interested in understanding the true reasons behind the economic challenges faced by Cuba should consider investigating the following topics:

1. Impact of corruption on the Cuban economy: A comprehensive study on the extent and consequences of corruption within the Cuban government and its impact on economic growth and development is essential. This research could shed light on the specific mechanisms through which corruption hampers economic progress.

2. Inflation and hyperinflation in Cuba: An examination of the root causes and long-term effects of inflation and hyperinflation in the Cuban economy would contribute to a better understanding of the challenges faced by the Cuban population and the government's ability to effectively manage the economy.

3. Economic impact of brain drain in Cuba: Investigating the economic consequences of the significant emigration of skilled professionals from Cuba could provide insights into the loss of human capital and its effects on economic growth and development.

4. Effects of centralized planning on the Cuban economy: A deeper analysis of the economic consequences of centralized planning in Cuba, including its impact on resource allocation, productivity, and innovation, would provide valuable insights into the limitations of this approach.

5. Cuban agriculture and food scarcity: Research focused on the challenges faced by the Cuban agricultural sector, including productivity issues, inefficiencies, and the impact on food scarcity, would contribute to the development of effective policies to address this critical issue.

6. Economic disparity and inequality in Cuba: Further exploration of the factors contributing to economic disparity and inequality in Cuba, including the role of government policies, could inform the design of more equitable economic systems.

7. Economic impact of limited foreign investment in Cuba: A study examining the economic consequences of limited foreign investment in Cuba, including the potential benefits and drawbacks, would provide insights into the importance of attracting foreign capital for economic growth and development.

8. Role of the black market and informal economy in Cuba: Investigating the size, dynamics, and economic impact of the black market and

informal economy in Cuba would enhance our understanding of the informal sector's role in the overall economy and its potential for growth and development.

9. Economic consequences of limited access to technology and the internet in Cuba: Research focusing on the economic implications of limited access to technology and the internet in Cuba would shed light on the barriers to technological advancement and innovation, and their impact on economic growth.

By exploring these research directions, scholars and economists can contribute to a more nuanced understanding of the economic challenges facing Cuba, moving beyond simplistic narratives and contributing to the development of effective policies for sustainable economic development.